THE GREAT STONES WAY

About the Author

Steve Davison is a freelance writer and photographer who has lived in Berkshire for over 25 years. He has written several guidebooks, as well as articles for a number of outdoor magazines and national and local newspapers, specialising in hill walking and UK and European travel, with interests in nature, geology and the countryside. A keen hill walker for many years and a Mountain Leader, Steve has also worked as a part-time outdoor education instructor. He is also a member of the Outdoor Writers and Photographers Guild. Find out more about him at www.steve-davison.co.uk.

Other Cicerone guides by the author

Walking in the Chilterns
The Ridgeway National Trail
Walking in the New Forest
Walking in the Thames Valley

THE GREAT STONES WAY

by Steve Davison

2 POLICE SQUARE, MILNTHORPE, CUMBRIA LA7 7PY
www.cicerone.co.uk

First edition 2014
ISBN: 978 1 85284 613 8

Printed by KHL Printing, Singapore
A catalogue record for this book is available from the British Library.
All photographs are by the author unless otherwise stated.

With thanks to Ian Ritchie and Jeff Goddard from The Friends of The
Ridgeway, for their help in checking the accuracy of this guide.

Advice to Readers

While every effort is made by our authors to ensure the accuracy of
guidebooks as they go to print, changes can occur during the lifetime of an
edition. If we know of any, there will be an Updates tab on this book's page
on the Cicerone website (www.cicerone.co.uk), so please check before
planning your trip. We also advise that you check information about such
things as transport, accommodation and shops locally. Even rights of way
can be altered over time. We are always grateful for information about
any discrepancies between a guidebook and the facts on the ground, sent
by email to info@cicerone.co.uk or by post to Cicerone, 2 Police Square,
Milnthorpe LA7 7PY, United Kingdom.

Front cover: The iconic stone circle at Stonehenge (Stage 5, Stonehenge loop)

CONTENTS

Route symbols on OS map extracts
(for OS legend see printed OS maps)

route

alternative route

start point

finish point

alternative finish point

route direction

Features on the overview map

County/Unitary boundary

Urban area

Area of Outstanding Natural Beauty

200m
75m
0m

GPX files

GPX files for all routes can be downloaded for free at www.cicerone.co.uk/member

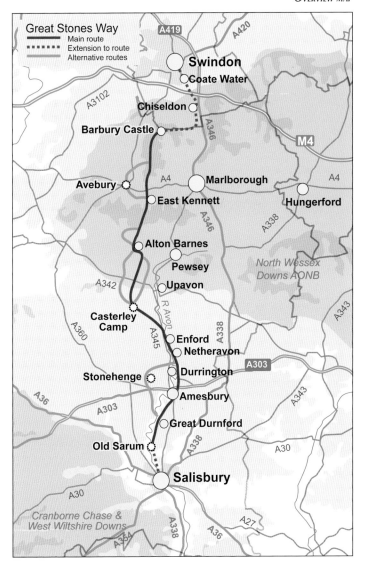

Sarsen stones in the stone circle at Avebury (Stage 2, Avebury loop)

INTRODUCTION

West Kennett Long Barrow – one of the largest Neolithic chambered tombs in Britain (Stage 2, Avebury loop)

Five thousand years ago, the rolling chalk landscape of Wiltshire between Swindon and Salisbury was, for more than a millennium, a scene of frenzied building work. Tracing a route through these now-peaceful downs and linking the greatest of England's prehistoric sites – Avebury and Stonehenge – the Great Stones Way takes you on a journey through this prehistoric landscape, passing Neolithic henges and stone circles, Bronze Age barrows and Iron Age hill forts. But that's not all, there are also ancient churches and the majestic medieval cathedral at Salisbury to visit along the way, as well as far-reaching views, tranquil riverside scenes, picturesque villages and cosy pubs to enjoy.

Take your time and enjoy the journey. Rest a while, listen to the sounds of the countryside around you, admire the views and imagine why our ancestors built these magnificent treasures.

This guidebook provides all the information needed to follow the Great Stones Way. Whether you do one continuous walk, or prefer to spread the pleasure over several visits, you are sure to enjoy your journey along this exciting and historic route.

THE GREAT STONES WAY

The Great Stones Way, a long-distance route opened in 2014, runs from Barbury Castle, near Swindon, to

9

Old Sarum, near Salisbury – a total of 58.5km (36½ miles) for the official route. However, the route described in this guide is longer – a maximum of 85.7km (53¼ miles), depending on the options taken – as it also includes an optional start at Coate Water; loops visiting Avebury, Alton Barnes White Horse and Stonehenge; and an optional finish at Salisbury. The route passes over comparatively gentle terrain, each stage having less than 250m of ascent (the greatest ascent being on Stages 1, 3 and 5).

The Great Stones Way follows existing rights of way and has been developed by The Friends of The Ridgeway, a registered charity that has campaigned for over 30 years to preserve the unique character of the ancient Ridgeway tracks that cross the chalk downs of Southern England, including The Ridgeway National Trail.

For further information about the Great Stones Way, visit www.great stonesway.org.uk.

HISTORY

The earliest inhabitants of the area were nomadic hunter-gatherers who travelled through the wooded landscape over 10,000 years ago. However, by the Neolithic period (4200–2200BC) a farming lifestyle was developing, permanent camps were being constructed and areas of land cleared for crops and animals. This was the period when the great monuments at Avebury and Stonehenge came into being. The Bronze Age (2200–750BC) saw further developments of these iconic sites as well as the building of numerous characteristic round barrows. During the Iron Age (750BC–AD43) defensive hill forts such as Barbury Castle and Old Sarum were built.

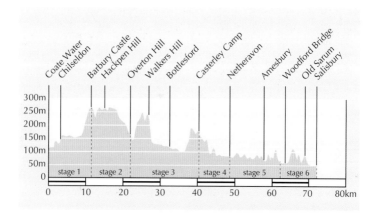

The Romans left little visible evidence in the region, although they did construct a road past Silbury Hill (now the A4) and built a town at Old Sarum. In the early part of the Anglo-Saxon period, following the demise of the Roman Empire in Britain around AD410, the Wansdyke – a massive linear earthwork across the Marlborough Downs above the Vale of Pewsey – was constructed. The Norman period (from 1066) was characterised by motte and bailey castles, such as the one at Old Sarum, as well as monasteries and churches with Romanesque rounded arches over windows and doorways; many churches in the area have their roots in the Norman period.

Prosperity and growth in the late 12th and 13th centuries led to the expansion of towns including Salisbury and the building of its impressive medieval cathedral. Much more recently transport improved with the opening of the Kennet and Avon Canal, quickly followed by the arrival of the railways. During the Second World War a number of airfields were built, including one at Alton Barnes, while Salisbury Plain was commandeered as a military training area, which still continues to this day.

GEOLOGY AND NATURE

The geology of the area is derived from the seas that once covered southern England and the sediments that were laid down at that time. The predominant feature – one that forms

Clockwise from top left: Yellow Vetch, Clustered Bellflower and Field Scabious

the rolling contours of the downs – is a thick layer of Upper Cretaceous chalk (99–65 million years ago), composed of incredible numbers of tiny fossil skeletons of algae, called coccoliths.

Associated with the chalk are irregular silica concretions known as flints. Our prehistoric ancestors used flint to make a range of tools, and it has also been widely used as a building material. A natural process of irregular hardening within the sandy beds that overlay the chalk produced blocks of tough sandstone that are more resistant to erosion. These are the famous sarsens that were used in the construction of the Neolithic stone circles at Avebury and Stonehenge; a great number of sarsens can be seen lying in the fields at Fyfield Down National Nature Reserve.

The Great Stones Way meanders through a patchwork of open chalk grassland, broadleaved woodland and farmland, and there are plenty of opportunities for catching glimpses of local wildlife including foxes, deer and the more elusive badger. During the summer, the open chalk grasslands are home to a myriad of butterflies and plants, as well as traditional farmland birds; high above, the silhouette of a buzzard might be seen. Along the rivers and waterways walkers will probably be accompanied by ducks and mute swans – or may be lucky enough to catch sight of the elusive otter or a flash of blue as a kingfisher speeds by.

PLANNING YOUR WALK

For your own enjoyment and convenience, plan your walk carefully in advance. This guide has been split into six stages ranging from 8.4km to 18.9km (see Appendix A for a route summary table). These are not intended to be individual day sections, but the start and end points coincide with places that offer parking, transport and accommodation facilities locally (see Appendix C for facilities near the route). The stages are provided to help walkers decide how far they would like to go each day – whether that means combining multiple stages or just undertaking part of a stage.

Stage 1 leaves the outskirts of Swindon and climbs up to the official start of the Great Stones Way at Barbury Castle, where the remains of an Iron Age hill fort offer commanding views. **Stage 2** (the first official section of the Great Stones Way) follows The Ridgeway National Trail south to Overton Hill; an alternative loop visits the remarkable prehistoric sites at Avebury, including the stone circle. **Stage 3**, an undulating stage, heads across the Vale of Pewsey (with a choice of three routes) to reach Casterley Camp on the edge of Salisbury Plain. On **Stage 4** the Great Stones Way drops down to meet the tranquil River Avon. The trail meanders along the valley on **Stage 5**, passing through several picturesque villages, and an optional loop visits Durrington Walls, Woodhenge and Stonehenge. **Stage 6** heads to the former Iron Age

The old diving platform at Coate Water just north of Swindon – starting point of Stage 1

hill fort at Old Sarum, later used by the Normans as a fortified castle, which marks the official end of the route. An optional end at Salisbury's medieval cathedral is also described.

A three-day schedule, following the Great Stones Way from Barbury Castle to Old Sarum (without the optional loops to Avebury and Stonehenge), could be planned as follows:

- **Day 1** Barbury Castle (Stage 2) to Honeystreet (Stage 3) (18.2km, 11¼ miles)
- **Day 2** Honeystreet to Netheravon or Haxton (Stage 4) (19.6km, 12¼ miles)
- **Day 3** Netheravon or Haxton to Old Sarum (Stage 6) (20.7km, 13 miles).

A four-day route from Coate Water to Salisbury, including the Avebury, Wansdyke and Stonehenge loops, might be planned as:

- **Day 1** Coate Water (Stage 1) to East Kennett (Stage 2) (26.1km, 16¼ miles)
- **Day 2** East Kennett to Netheravon or Haxton (Stage 4) (28.9km, 18 miles)
- **Day 3** Netheravon or Haxton to Great Durnford (Stage 5) (18.1km, 11¼ miles)
- **Day 4** Great Durnford to Salisbury (Stage 6) (10.4km, 6½ miles).

GETTING TO AND FROM THE WAY

The nearest mainline train station to the start of the route is Swindon, on the line from London Paddington to the south-west and south Wales. Local buses operate daily between Swindon town centre and Coate Water (east-bound stop) or Chiseldon. National Express coaches (403) running between London Victoria and

After passing the Wansdyke, the route heads for Walkers Hill (Stage 3)

Bath stop at Coate Water (A4259). (Stage 1 in this guide details a walking route from Coate Water to Barbury Castle – the official start of the Great Stones Way.)

Salisbury, located a few kilometres south of the official end of the Great Stones Way at Old Sarum (which has daily bus services to Salisbury), has rail services on the line between London Waterloo and the south-west. (A walking route to Salisbury from the final section of the Great Stones Way is described in Stage 6.)

Between Swindon and Salisbury (between Pewsey and Salisbury on Sundays), Salisbury Reds (www.salisburyreds.co.uk) operate route X5. This follows the A346 south to Marlborough, calling at Chiseldon, and then follows the A345 to Salisbury with intermediate stops

including Enford, Netheravon, Figheldean, Bulford, Durrington, Amesbury and Old Sarum (on Stages 4, 5 and 6).

Contact details for public transport information are given in Appendix B.

For anyone wishing to drive, there is parking (either car park or on street) available at the start and end of each stage. Always remember to park considerately, and be aware that theft from parked cars does occur, so do not leave anything valuable in your car.

WHEN TO WALK

The route can be undertaken at any time of the year, although walking between early spring and the end of autumn offers the chance of more settled weather and better walking conditions.

WHERE TO STAY

Accommodation ranges from campsites to B&Bs, pubs with rooms and hotels, and places where accommodation may be available are given in the box at the start of each stage description. Some of these places are located along the route, while others involve short detours (less than 3km) off route.

A brief list of some accommodation close to the route is given in Appendix D, and up-to-date details are available from local tourist information offices (see Appendix B).

FOOD AND DRINK

Places where refreshments and food may be available (pubs, cafés and shops) are mentioned in the box at the start of each stage description (some of these are located along the route, while others involve short detours (less than 3km) off route). A table in Appendix C also gives an overview of where refreshments are available along the route. However, there is no guarantee that any particular establishment will be open when required, and walkers should carry enough food and water for the day with them.

WAYMARKING, ACCESS AND RIGHTS OF WAY

The Great Stones Way follows signed rights of way and, at the time of publication, parts of the route have also been signed using the Great Stones Way logo. The descriptions in this guide, along with the map extracts and the signage on the ground, mean

(L) Great Stones Way route marker and (R) Ridgeway National Trail signpost (followed on Stage 2)

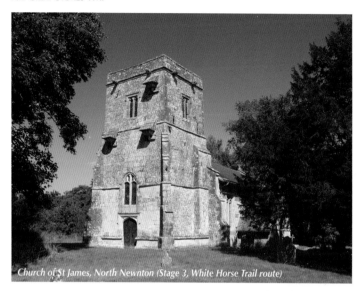

Church of St James, North Newnton (Stage 3, White Horse Trail route)

that route finding should not cause any major problems; however, it is recommended that walkers also carry the relevant Ordnance Survey Explorer map.

Rights of way are indicated on signage as follows:

- **Footpaths** Yellow arrow – walkers only
- **Bridleways** Blue arrow – walkers, cyclists and horse riders
- **Restricted byways** Purple arrow – walkers, cyclists, horse riders and carriage drivers
- **Byways** Red arrow – same as for restricted byways plus motorcycles and motorised vehicles.

USING THIS GUIDE

In this guidebook an information box at the start of each stage gives the stage start and finish location accompanied by grid references, stage distance, map details, places close to the route that offer refreshments (pubs, cafés and shops), public transport links and accommodation.

A short introduction gives a brief overview of the stage, identifying any major points of interest, including towns and villages. Throughout the route text easily identifiable features that appear on the OS map are highlighted in **bold** to help with navigation, and there is information given about places of interest en route.

Distances and times

The distances given in the text (metric, with approximate imperial conversions where appropriate) have been measured from OS Explorer maps. The walking time for each stage is based on a walking speed of 4km per hour (2½ miles per hour), plus 10 minutes for every 100m of ascent. This is the minimum amount of walking time required to undertake the stage and does not include any time for rests, photography, consulting the map or guidebook, visits or simply admiring the view – all of which can add substantially to the day's activity.

GPX files for all the stages of this route are available to download free from the Cicerone website at www.cicerone.co.uk/member.

Maps

The OS maps covering the Great Stones Way are
• Landranger (1:50,000): 173 and 184
• Explorer (1:25,000): 169 (Stage 1 only), 157 and 130.

This guide contains extracts of the OS 1:50,000 Landranger series of maps with information added to show the main route and any alternative routes.

Taking care

When out walking, please respect the countryside and follow the Countryside Code:
• be safe – plan ahead and follow any signs
• leave gates and property as you find them

The Kennet and Avon Canal at Honeystreet (Stage 3)

A great spot to take a seat and admire the views across the River Avon valley before moving on to Old Sarum (Stage 6)

- protect plants and animals, and take your litter home
- keep dogs under close control
- consider other people.

The Great Stones Way passes a number of scheduled monuments that may be easily damaged without due care, so:

- do not disturb, walk over, damage, use metal detectors on, or remove any objects from any scheduled monument sites
- always follow marked routes.

Finally, always take great care when either walking along, or crossing, roads and railway tracks.

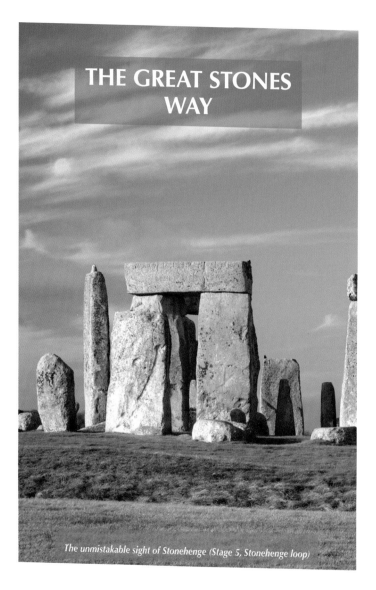

THE GREAT STONES WAY

The unmistakable sight of Stonehenge (Stage 5, Stonehenge loop)

STAGE 1
Coate Water to Barbury Castle (official start)

Start	Coate Water Country Park (SU 177 827; parking), off the A4259, just north of junction 15 of the M4
Finish	Barbury Castle Country Park car park (SU 157 760)
Distance	11.3km (7 miles)
Ascent	245m
Time	3¼hrs
Maps	OS Explorer 169 and 157
Refreshments	Pubs and shops at Swindon and Chiseldon; café at Coate Water
Public transport	Swindon has a rail station with local bus links (daily) to Coate Water (east-bound stop; SU 176 830); National Express buses (403) between London and Bath stop at Coate Water (SU 180 828); bus links to Chiseldon (SU 187 797) from Swindon (X5/70)
Accommodation	Swindon – wide choice; Chiseldon

The first stage, which is not part of the official route, is provided to allow walkers using public transport an easy access route to the official start at Barbury Castle. From Coate Water, on the outskirts of Swindon, the route passes through Chiseldon and follows part of an old railway that used to run between Swindon and Marlborough. After leaving the former railway, the route heads west up over Burderop Down.

Walkers **arriving by bus** at the Coate Water east-bound stop on Queen's Drive should follow the path south through two underpasses and continue to Coate Water. From the long-distance bus stop head west, turn left along Day House Lane for 200m, then right (cycle route 45) to Coate Water.

From the northern edge of the lake at **Coate Water Country Park** head east and follow the waterside path as it curves right (south). A path to the left leads to the Richard Jefferies Museum.

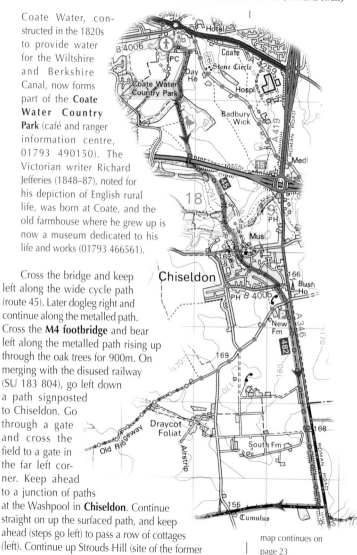

Coate Water, constructed in the 1820s to provide water for the Wiltshire and Berkshire Canal, now forms part of the **Coate Water Country Park** (café and ranger information centre, 01793 490150). The Victorian writer Richard Jefferies (1848–87), noted for his depiction of English rural life, was born at Coate, and the old farmhouse where he grew up is now a museum dedicated to his life and works (01793 466561).

Cross the bridge and keep left along the wide cycle path (route 45). Later dogleg right and continue along the metalled path. Cross the **M4 footbridge** and bear left along the metalled path rising up through the oak trees for 900m. On merging with the disused railway (SU 183 804), go left down a path signposted to Chiseldon. Go through a gate and cross the field to a gate in the far left corner. Keep ahead to a junction of paths at the Washpool in **Chiseldon**. Continue straight on up the surfaced path, and keep ahead (steps go left) to pass a row of cottages (left). Continue up Strouds Hill (site of the former

map continues on page 23

21

rail station) to a junction (shop/newsagent to the right) and head up Station Road (bus stop for services from Swindon) to a junction with New Street (B4005).

Chiseldon is located at the head of a coombe with springs (the Washpool) overlooked by the former Iron Age hill forts of Liddington and Barbury Castle; the Saxon name Ceosel Dene means 'stony valley'. In 2004 the Chiseldon Cauldrons, a unique collection of 12 Iron Age cooking pots or cauldrons (Europe's largest such collection), was discovered nearby. The railway arrived in 1881 with the opening of the Swindon, Marlborough and Andover Railway; the line closed in 1961, and part of the disused track-bed now forms the Chiseldon and Marlborough Railway Path. From 1914 until 1960 the parish was home to Chiseldon Camp (now demolished), which originally opened to train soldiers for the First World War.

After leaving the Chiseldon and Marlborough Railway Path the route heads west towards Barbury Castle

Heading west up Burderop Down

Cross the **B4005** and take the cycle path opposite to reach a minor road; ahead on the left is the Three Trees farm shop and café (01793 741436), whilst 700m west along the B4005 is The Patriot Arms (01793 740331) and village shop. ▶ Cross over and follow the old railway line (cycle route 482) south, running parallel to the **A346** for 3km.

At the crossing byway (SU 197 766) turn right, after 1.2km cross a minor road and

The road to the right later becomes a track (byway) known as Old Ridgeway (cycle route 45) that joins The Ridgeway just west of Barbury Castle at SU 145 763.

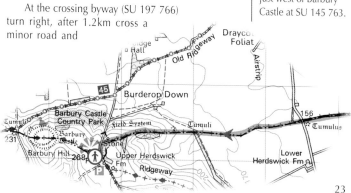

The memorial stone on Burderop Down looking towards Liddington Castle

continue westwards to a crossing bridleway (SU 170 763). Bear right and then fork left through scrub, go through a gate and follow the left-hand field margin up Burderop Down. Cross a stile and continue alongside the fence; to the right are far-reaching views and later a sarsen stone with plaques.

This stone commemorates two local writers – **Richard Jefferies** (mentioned earlier) and **Alfred Williams** (1877–1930). Williams was dubbed 'the hammerman poet' as he used to work in the Great Western Railway factory at Swindon.

Leave through a gate, turn left up the minor road for 125m and then right to the car park at **Barbury Castle Country Park**.

STAGE 2
Barbury Castle to Overton Hill

Start	Barbury Castle Country Park car park (SU 157 760)
Finish	Overton Hill car park on A4 (SU 118 680)
Distance	10.5km (6½ miles) or (Avebury loop) 14.1km (8¾ miles)
Ascent	80m or (Avebury loop) 115m
Time	2¾hrs or (Avebury loop) 3¾hrs
Maps	OS Explorer 157
Refreshments	Pubs at Avebury, Beckhampton and West Overton; shop at Avebury
Public transport	Daily bus service (route 49) from Swindon calls at Avebury (SU 102 699); National Express buses (402) between London and Frome stop at Beckhampton (SU 089 689)
Accommodation	Avebury, Avebury Trusloe, Beckhampton and East Kennett

The first stage of the Great Stones Way follows the Ridgeway National Trail from the lofty heights of Barbury Castle southwards to Overton Hill. On the way it visits the Hackpen Hill White Horse and passes near the sarsen-strewn landscape of the Fyfield Downs National Nature Reserve. Alternatively, walkers can take a loop through Avebury that passes the world-renowned stone circle and henge and other impressive prehistoric sites.

Head north-west through the car park at **Barbury Castle Country Park**, passing the toilet block, and pass through

The impressive earthworks of Barbury Castle (Iron Age hill fort) mark the official start of the Great Stones Way

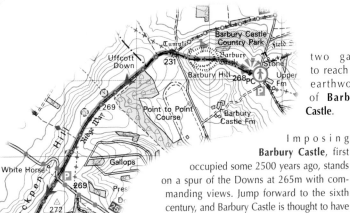

two gates to reach the earthworks of **Barbury Castle**.

Imposing **Barbury Castle**, first occupied some 2500 years ago, stands on a spur of the Downs at 265m with commanding views. Jump forward to the sixth century, and Barbury Castle is thought to have been where the Britons were defeated at the Battle of Beranburgh (Beran Byrig) in AD556. To the north, below the Downs, is the former Second World War Wroughton Airfield; the hangars are now part of the British Science Museum.

Go through the centre of the hill fort to the western edge (a detour along the ramparts gives some great views) and follow the track down to a lane. Turn right and continue for 40m, then go left up a short rise before following the track to a car park (SU 129 747) and minor road, passing three picturesque circular beech copses on the way. Cross over and follow the track over **Hackpen Hill**.

The gate on the right gives access to the **Hackpen Hill White Horse** cut by Henry Eatwell, Parish Clerk of Broad Hinton and a local publican, to commemorate the coronation of Queen Victoria in 1838.

After a dogleg, where the White Horse Trail forks left, there is a seat with a view west towards the Lansdowne Monument on Cherhill Down. Continue southwards to a cross-junction at SU 124 708; right heads to Avebury (see below) and left heads across Overton Down to the sarsen-strewn landscape of Fyfield Down National Nature Reserve (NNR) (700m each way). The Great Stones Way goes straight on to the car park at **Overton Hill** (SU 118 680).

On the left are several early **Bronze Age burial mounds** or round barrows (about 2000BC). Much later a **Roman road** between Cunetio (near Marlborough) and Verlicio (near Chippenham) passed through here.

Avebury loop

Leave the Great Stones Way at SU 124 708 and turn right down the Herepath or Green Street (also known as the **Wessex Ridgeway**) to reach the centre of **Avebury**, passing through the henge earthworks. At the main road keep ahead past The Red Lion (01672 539266) and follow the High Street south-west. Some 50m after

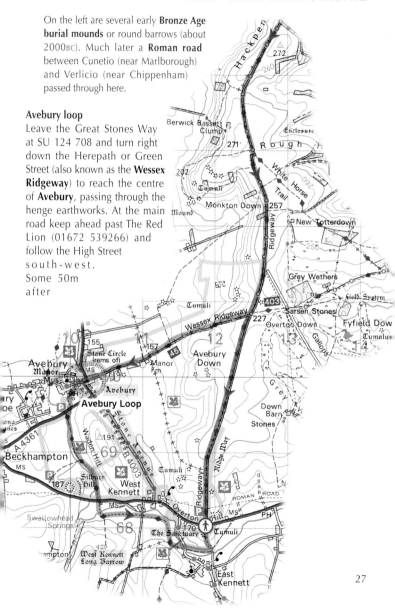

27

the village shop turn left along the enclosed path. A track to the right leads to Avebury Manor and the Alexander Keiller Museum, and further along the High Street is St James' Church which, although altered by the Normans, still retains its tall Anglo-Saxon nave.

The **Avebury henge** and associated sites, together with Stonehenge, have been designated a World Heritage Site. The most impressive feature at Avebury, the large henge, is a type of Neolithic earthwork, dating from 2600BC, consisting of a circular outer bank and inner ditch (a defensive hill fort has an outer ditch and inner bank). Within this structure is the outer stone circle, one of Europe's

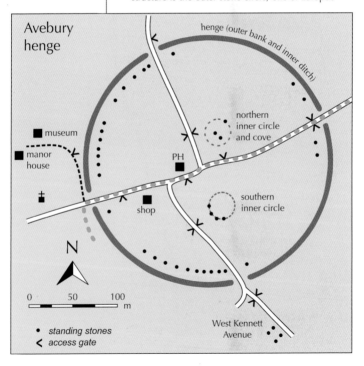

Avebury henge

henge (outer bank and inner ditch)

- museum
- manor house
- PH
- northern inner circle and cove
- southern inner circle
- shop

N

0   50   100
m

West Kennett Avenue

- • standing stones
- ‹ access gate

largest stone circles, originally marked with 98 sarsen stones, along with two smaller inner stone circles and part of the present village. Linking the henge with The Sanctuary (see Stage 3) is the 2.5km long West Kennett Avenue, which originally consisted of 100 pairs of standing stones.

The Alexander Keiller Museum is named after Alexander Keiller (1889–1955), heir to the

One of the sarsen stones that make up the stone circle

Dundee-based marmalade business, who was responsible for excavating many of the sites at Avebury in the 1930s. The museum houses archaeological finds from the area. Nearby is the Manor House, once the home of Alexander Keiller, which dates from 16th century (01672 539250).

Keep ahead through the car park and turn right along the **A4361** for 40m. Turn left across the road and go through the gate. Keep to the path beside the River Kennet for 1.3km. Over to the right is the unmistakable outline of Silbury Hill (there is no access to the hill).

The 40m high **Silbury Hill** is the largest man-made prehistoric mound in Europe, built some time around 2400BC (late Neolithic), at a similar time to the Avebury stone circle. No one really knows why it was built, although local legend attributes the mound to the devil. He was planning to dump a load of earth on nearby Marlborough, but was stopped by the priests at Avebury, while in another version it's a cobbler who thwarts the devil.

The unique outline of Silbury Hill

With care, cross the **A4** and turn left. Continue for 30m and then go right through the gate following a track southwards. After crossing the River Kennet bear left along a path to a large oak tree (SU 104 681); here a 400m detour to the right (south) leads to the West Kennett Long Barrow.

West Kennett Long Barrow

> **West Kennett Long Barrow** is one of the largest and most impressive Neolithic chambered tombs in Britain, dating from 3600BC. During excavations the partial remains of at least 46 individuals, along with pottery, beads and stone implements, were found.

Follow the fence along the left edge of the field to a stile and continue along the track. Cross the lane and stile to follow the hedge on the right as it curves right to a stile. Cross over and follow the tree-shaded path to a track and turn left to a minor road. Go left over the bridge and immediately right following the right-hand field margin to a junction at SU 119 676 and rejoin the Great Stones Way. Some 400m to the left is **Overton Hill** car park and The Sanctuary, and the onward route curves right towards East Kennett (accommodation).

31

STAGE 3
Overton Hill to Casterley Camp

Start	Overton Hill car park (SU 118 680)
Finish	Casterley Camp car park (SU 112 536)
Distance	18.9km (11¾ miles); Alton Barnes White Horse route: add 2.4km (1½ miles); Marden Henge route: add 1.2km (¾ mile); White Horse Trail route: add 2.1km (1½ miles)
Ascent	330m; Alton Barnes White Horse route: add 50m; Marden Henge route: minus 15m; White Horse Trail route: add 5m
Time	5¼hrs; Alton Barnes White Horse route: add ½hr; Marden Henge route: add ¼hr; White Horse Trail route: add ½hr
Maps	OS Explorer 157 and 130
Refreshments	Pub and café at Honeystreet; pub at Bottlesford (Wilcot, North Newnton and Upavon – off route)
Public transport	Avebury (see Stage 2); off route – North Newnton (SU 132 570) and Upavon (SU 134 550) have daily buses to Swindon and Salisbury (X5)
Accommodation	Avebury and surrounding villages, Honeystreet, Bottlesford (Wilcot, North Newnton, Rushall and Upavon – off route)

The Great Stones Way continues south past The Sanctuary and through East Kennett before steadily climbing the chalk downs, passing through the earthworks of the Wansdyke on the way. From the top of the downs a great view extends across the Vale of Pewsey to Salisbury Plain. After dropping down through Alton Barnes and Alton Priors the route arrives at the Kennet and Avon Canal. Here there is a choice of three, equally interesting, onwards routes to Casterley Camp – via the Great Stones Way, Marden Henge or the White Horse Trail.

The alternative Avebury loop rejoins here.

From **Overton Hill** car park head south, carefully crossing the A4, and take the track opposite, passing just left of The Sanctuary to a junction at SU 119 676. ◄

The Sanctuary, which dates from 3000BC, consisted of concentric timber and stone circles. We know from the writings of John Aubrey that in 1648 many of the stones were still standing; however, within 100 years the site was destroyed (the stones, like many others at ancient sites, were used as a source of building material). All that remains today are concrete blocks marking where the timbers and stones once stood.

Bear left and right along the track, cross the River Kennet and keep ahead at two road junctions through **East Kennett**. At the last house on the right (where the road curves left), fork right on a track (byway) towards Manor Farm. After 300m fork left following the track up **Lurkeley Hill** for 2km – from here the view north-west includes Silbury Hill – to pass through the tree-shaded remains of the Wansdyke (SU 118 648).

The **Wansdyke**, a linear earthwork that stretches west across the Marlborough Downs above the Vale of Pewsey from Marlborough to Morgan's Hill, dates back to Saxon times.

Keep to the track ahead to follow the main route. Alternatively, take a detour that follows the Wansdyke and visits a 19th-century white horse before rejoining the main route.

Wansdyke and Alton Barnes White Horse route

Turn right (westwards) along the Wansdyke Path for 1.6km to reach a track with a view of the earthwork stretching out across the downs (SU 102 646). Turn left through a gate to enter Pewsey

map continues on page 37

33

The Alton Barnes White Horse above the Vale of Pewsey

Downs NNR (information board) and follow the White Horse Trail (white horse logo) as it contours south and east before passing above the Alton Barnes White Horse to reach a col just west of **Adam's Grave,** a Neolithic long barrow or burial mound (SU 111 635).

> The **Alton Barnes White Horse**, visible from the Vale of Pewsey and the northern edge of Salisbury Plain, was commissioned by Robert Pile in 1812.

Here rejoin the Great Stones Way by turning right.

On the skyline of nearby Knap Hill are the earthworks of a Neolithic causewayed camp dating from around 3500BC.

Walkers who don't take the detour follow the track down through three fields (fence on left) to a road with a **car park** opposite (SU 115 638). ◄ Do not join the road but go through the gate and follow the permissive path southwards through the field. Go through a gate on the right and bear half-left (south-west) up **Walkers Hill**, passing through a gate on the way to reach a slight col (SU 111 635) just to the right of **Adam's Grave** (a Neolithic long barrow or burial mound). The path to the west-north-west leads to the Alton Barnes White Horse (500m each way).

STAGE 3 – OVERTON HILL TO CASTERLEY CAMP

▶ After admiring the view across the Vale of Pewsey, follow a good path southwards (with slope down to the right; Adam's Grave to the left) from the col for 400m before turning left over the ridge (open access land) down to a gate and stile. Cross over and turn right down the road for 100m (care required), then left through a field entrance (bridleway).

Follow the tree-shaded bridleway (Ridge Way) down-hill, later passing a house to arrive at a lane in **Alton Priors**. Go left, then right past an old thatched barn (the sarsen stone on the village green has a cut-out of Alton Barnes White Horse) to the lane end. Go through the turnstile and head across the field, keeping right of the church to the trees. ▶

> Pop inside the Norman **All Saints Church**, cared for by the Churches Conservation Trust, to see some fine Jacobean carved wooden choir stalls, a tomb-chest of William Button (died 1590), and two sarsen stones hidden under trapdoors in the floor. These may be from an earlier sacred site – early Christian churches were sometimes built on existing religious sites. Outside in the churchyard stands an ancient yew tree (another pagan symbol) said to be well over 1000 years old.

Keep to the cobbled path through two turnstiles and across footbridges to a path junction in the middle of the next field. Turn left and leave through a gate with the church on the left, then turn right along the lane through **Alton Barnes**.

> The **Church of St Mary the Virgin** dates back to Saxon times. Call in to see the 16th-century tie-beamed and wind-braced roof, a Georgian gallery and some interesting monuments.

At the T-junction turn left along the road towards **Honeystreet**. After 200m a field entrance on the right gives access to a memorial stone on the last remaining

The detour via the white horse rejoins the main route here.

To visit the church go left at the path junction.

35

All Saints Church,
Alton Priors

The Barge Inn (01672 851705) is 300m to the west. Honeystreet Café (01672 851232) is at the wharf just before the bridge.

air-raid shelter (SU 104 617) at the former RAF Alton Barnes (Second World War). Cross the **Kennet and Avon Canal** and immediately turn right to join the towpath. ◀

> The **Kennet and Avon Canal** opened in 1810 connecting Bristol to the River Thames at Reading. However, the opening of the Great Western Railway brought about its gradual decline. Fortunately, after years of neglect, the canal has now been fully restored.

> From here, there is a choice of three routes to the car park at Casterley Camp. The Great Stones Way route is described below, followed by the alternative Marden Henge and White Horse Trail routes.

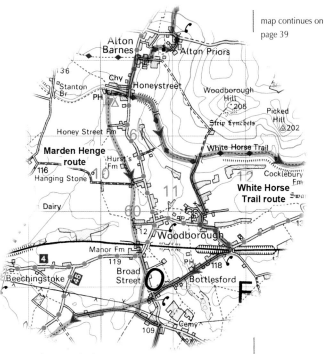

map continues on page 39

To keep with the Great Stones Way turn right (east) under the bridge and follow the canal for 1.4km to another bridge. ▶ Leave the canal (the White Horse Trail route, below, continues straight on along the canal) and turn right along the track to **Woodborough**. At Church Farm a squeeze-stile on the right gives access to St Mary Magdalene Church; originally from the 13th century, it was rebuilt in 1850.

Once past the farm, follow the lane to the right, then go left at the next two junctions. At the next junction go right (road to Bottlesford and Hilcott) and cross the railway bridge. Keep right for 1.2km through **Bottlesford**, passing The Seven Stars pub (01672 851325), to a cross-junction.

Go straight on, following Gores Lane past houses to a crossing bridleway, then turn left, passing under the

On the way, a stile on the right gives access to a memorial commemorating the crew of an Albemarle Bomber that crashed nearby in 1944.

power lines. Turn left along Yard's Lane to a crossroads at **Hilcott** and go right (south) following Wilsford Road for 1.5km to **Cuttenham Farm**. At the right-hand bend, fork left (straight on) on a signed bridleway and, where this turns left, go straight on through a gate heading south towards the trees, soon crossing the infant River Avon via a footbridge.

Continue along the field margin, passing under the power lines to reach the A342 beside **Coombe Cottage**. Cross over and keep ahead along the left-hand field margin, later heading steeply uphill (look back for a view across the Vale of Pewsey) to a byway on the edge of Salisbury Plain training area. Turn left and continue for 1.8km to the parking area at **Casterley Camp**. The track at SU 107 540 heads to Rushall (2.5km), and the metalled track north-east from the car park heads to Upavon (2.6km; bus services) – both offer accommodation.

Salisbury Plain, an expansive area of chalk grassland, has been used by the Ministry of Defence since 1898 for training purposes. Some restricted areas are still used for live firing practice – you'll

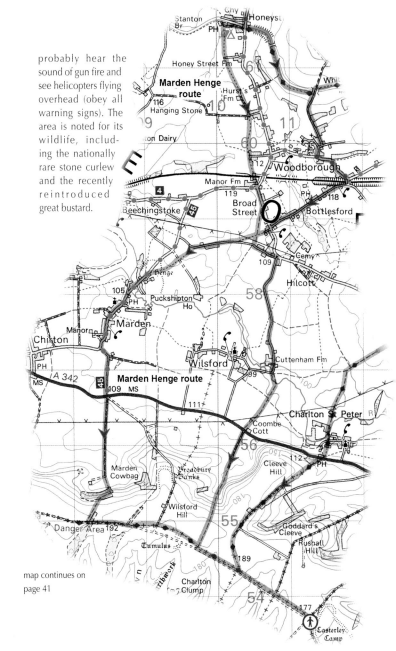

probably hear the sound of gun fire and see helicopters flying overhead (obey all warning signs). The area is noted for its wildlife, including the nationally rare stone curlew and the recently reintroduced great bustard.

Marden Henge route

Marden Henge route

map continues on page 41

Marden Henge route

Turn left (west) and walk alongside the canal to The Barge Inn (01672 851705), then turn left to the entrance road and go straight over a stile. Continue southwards alongside the fence, cross a stile and keep ahead through three fields, crossing a farm track on the way. Continue along the enclosed path and track at **Hurst's Farm**. At the corner, keep ahead and slightly left up steps and continue through the field following the right-hand hedge to the corner. Go right and then left in the next field following the left-hand boundary through three fields, and later keep ahead to a stile. With great care cross the **railway** (follow signs to crossing point) and leave via another stile. Continue across the grass and through some trees to a road junction at **Broad Street**.

Go straight on (southwards) along the road for Pewsey and Upavon, and after 350m fork right (opposite Swallowtails) following a track with houses on the left. Continue along the left-hand field boundary, fork right on a crossing path, pass under power lines and bear right along the road for 500m. Shortly after **Puckshipton Dairy** fork left and head diagonally across the field towards the trees. Cross stiles and a surfaced track and continue through two fields to a road, passing through the earthworks of a henge.

> This large **henge** monument dates from the late Neolithic (2400–2000BC) period; unfortunately the earthworks have been damaged by ploughing and general erosion.

Follow the road for 1.2km through **Marden**, passing The Millstream pub (01380 848490) and the 12th-century All Saints Church (inside are some fine Norman ornamentation and colourful stained-glass windows) to a Y-junction. Fork left, cross the **A342** to a track and take the right-hand fork straight on (south) uphill. Bear right and left at the trees of Marden Copse to reach the edge of Salisbury Plain training area. Turn left (south-east) and continue for 3.3km to the car park at **Casterley Camp**.

White Horse Trail route

Turn right (east) under the bridge, keeping with the Great Stones Way at first, and follow the canal for 1.4km to another bridge. Continue along the towpath for a further 1.6km to another bridge (Ladies Bridge – SU 128 606); 1.6km straight on is Wilcot – pub and accommodation. Turn right past **Cocklebury Farm** and

map continues on page 43

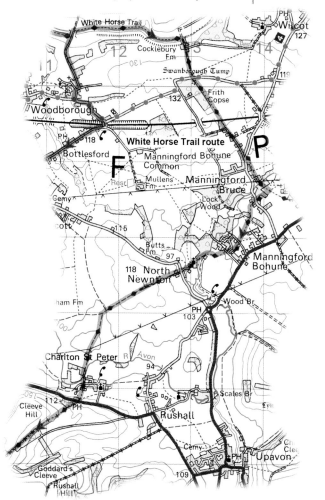

41

Alfred the Great met up with his brother, Ethelred, here on their way to fight the invading Danes in AD871.

continue along the driveway to a road, opposite the **Swanborough Tump**. ◄

Cross over and continue straight on following the right-hand field margin. With great care cross the **railway** and keep ahead, soon following a track (Dragon Lane) past houses to the main street in **Manningford Bruce**. Turn sharp left to Gable Cottage, then right along the bridleway following the left-hand field margin; continue straight on along the enclosed path. Keep ahead past the building, crossing several footbridges over the River Avon, and enter the field through a gate. Fork right and continue for 100m, then turn right over a stile. Continue through the trees, crossing a footbridge and stile, and head across the field to a lane at **Manningford Bohune**.

Go straight over, following the enclosed path between houses to a field. Aim half-left (south) across the field, cross a stile and footbridge at the trees, and continue through two fields (stiles) to a lane. Cross slightly left and follow the enclosed path, then track past the buildings to a junction. Turn right and continue for a few metres, then go left following the right-hand field margin. At the trout farm keep to the right-hand track for 25m and fork right along a path with the River Avon on the right. Later turn right over a footbridge, continue past the 13th-century Church of St James and then head along the lane to a road junction in **North Newnton**. ◄

600m to the left along the road is The Woodbridge Inn (01980 630266), which is also on a bus route.

Cross over, go through the farmyard and follow the track for 1.2km, passing some farm buildings. Keep left at two junctions, following the hedge-lined bridleway south towards **Charlton St Peter**.

The early 18th-century poet Stephen Duck, who wrote 'The Thresher's Labour', was born in the village and the annual 'Duck Feast' held in early June celebrates his life and work.

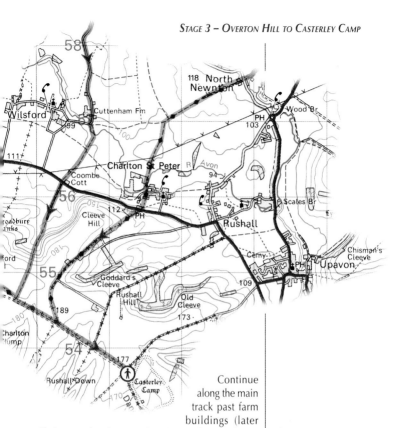

Continue along the main track past farm buildings (later metalled) to reach a four-way junction. ▶ Go straight on, passing between a house (left) and barn (right). Keep ahead up through fields to reach the **A342**. Cross over and take the track opposite, heading uphill for 2km. Keep ahead at the junction to pass a trig point and reach the edge of Salisbury Plain training area. Turn left and continue for 1.2km to the car park at **Casterley Camp**.

About 150m to the left is St Peter's Church, which dates from the 12th century.

43

STAGE 4
Casterley Camp to Netheravon

Start	Casterley Camp car park (SU 112 536)
Finish	Netheravon High Street (SU 147 490)
Distance	8.4km (5¼ miles)
Ascent	100m
Time	2¼hrs
Maps	OS Explorer 130
Refreshments	Pubs at Longstreet and Netheravon
Public transport	Buses between Swindon and Salisbury (X5) follow the A345, stopping at Upavon and West Chisenbury (detours), Enford (SU 139 515) and Netheravon (SU 147 490)
Accommodation	(Rushall, Upavon and East Chisenbury – off route), Haxton

A short stage from Casterley Camp drops down from the edge of Salisbury Plain to the more tranquil surroundings of the River Avon, passing through picturesque Enford and Longstreet to arrive at Netheravon.

From the car park head south-east along the gravel track, with the remains of **Casterley Camp** on the left. Soon fork left at a waymarker and head south-east across open grass.

After leaving Casterley Camp the Great Stones Way heads across open fields

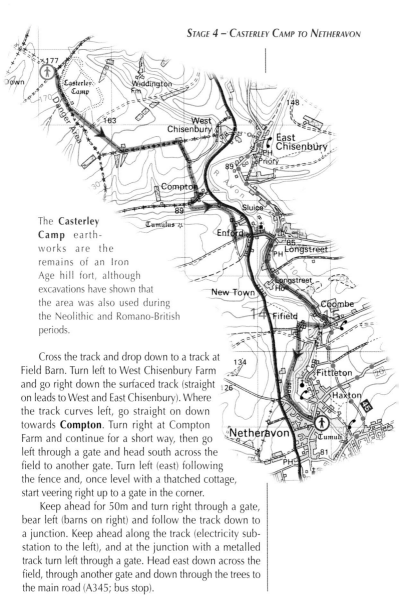

The **Casterley Camp** earthworks are the remains of an Iron Age hill fort, although excavations have shown that the area was also used during the Neolithic and Romano-British periods.

Cross the track and drop down to a track at Field Barn. Turn left to West Chisenbury Farm and go right down the surfaced track (straight on leads to West and East Chisenbury). Where the track curves left, go straight on down towards **Compton**. Turn right at Compton Farm and continue for a short way, then go left through a gate and head south across the field to another gate. Turn left (east) following the fence and, once level with a thatched cottage, start veering right up to a gate in the corner.

Keep ahead for 50m and turn right through a gate, bear left (barns on right) and follow the track down to a junction. Keep ahead along the track (electricity sub-station to the left), and at the junction with a metalled track turn left through a gate. Head east down across the field, through another gate and down through the trees to the main road (A345; bus stop).

45

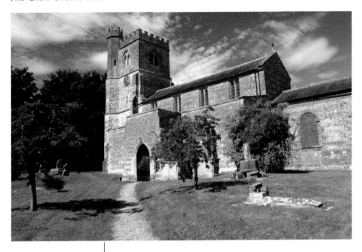

All Saints Church, Enford

Cross over and follow the minor road down through **Enford**, passing All Saints Church (left), then crossing the River Avon to a T-junction.

> **Enford**, mentioned in a Saxon charter dated AD934, when land was given to Winchester Cathedral by King Aethelstan, is home to the Norman All Saints Church, which incorporates parts of an earlier building. The River Avon – a classic chalk river – is met several times on this route. It rises at both Devizes and Pewsey before merging at Upavon and then continuing southwards to the English Channel.

Turn right (left leads to East Chisenbury) and carefully follow the lane for 1.5km through **Longstreet**, home to some picturesque thatched cottages including The Swan Inn (01980 670338), to a junction in **Coombe** (SU 150 503). Turn right along the surfaced path, cross the footbridge over the River Avon and keep ahead to **Fifield**.

Follow the lane as it curves left, and at the right-hand bend go straight on along the track. Cross over the tank

track and keep ahead, soon following the trees on the left. Continue along the valley, following the boundary on the left, and later keep straight on along the track towards Netheravon, with the River Avon and Fittleton's church on the left. Bear left (straight on) along the minor road (Mill Road), passing the Stonehenge Ales brewery, to a T-junction and turn right to **Netheravon** High Street (shop and bus stop). Haxton (accommodation) is 250m to the left across the River Avon.

The River Avon between Coombe and Fifield

> **Netheravon** is home to All Saints Church, parts of which date back to late Saxon times. The author Frank Sawyer (1906–80), who designed the Pheasant Tail Nymph for fly fishing and wrote *Keeper of the Stream* and *Nymphs and the Trout*, spent much of his life in Netheravon as river keeper on the Avon. Just to the east is Netheravon Airfield, said to be the longest continuously operating airfield in the world, having been used by the Royal Flying Corps (forerunner of the Royal Air Force) since before the First World War.

STAGE 5
Netheravon to Great Durnford

Start	Netheravon High Street (SU 147 490)
Finish	Great Durnford – The Black Horse pub (SU 134 379)
Distance	13.9km (8¾ miles) or (Stonehenge loop) 18.1km (11¼ miles)
Ascent	220m or (Stonehenge loop) 245m
Time	4hrs or (Stonehenge loop) 5hrs
Maps	OS Explorer 130
Refreshments	Pubs and shops at Netheravon, Durrington, Larkhill, Bulford and Amesbury; pub at Great Durnford
Public transport	Buses between Swindon and Salisbury (X5) stop at Netheravon (SU 147 490), Figheldean (SU 151 468), Durrington (SU 151 440), Larkhill (SU 143 440), Bulford (SU 167 435) and Amesbury bus station (SU 155 413)
Accommodation	Haxton, Durrington, Bulford, Amesbury and Great Durnford

From Netheravon the route continues along the Avon, passing through Bulford and Amesbury to arrive at Great Durnford. An alternative loop, bypassing Amesbury, takes walkers on a journey through history, passing Durrington Walls, Woodhenge and Stonehenge, as well as numerous burial mounds, before rejoining the Great Stones Way near Great Durnford.

Straight on leads to the church and a view of an early 18th-century dovecote which contains 700 chalk nesting boxes (no access to the field).

Head south along **Netheravon** High Street for 500m to a junction with a central tree and circular seat, then fork left (right goes to the A345 and the Dog and Gun pub – 01980 671287). ◄ Follow the road across the **River Avon**, and where the road curves left at Choulston Farm bear half-right through a gate. Head south-east across the field, passing a sewage works (left) and small copse (right) before following the field boundary to a gate. Turn right along the lane to a junction and fork right towards **Figheldean**.

The **Church of St Michael and All Angels** in Figheldean, which has an original Norman tower and 15th-century Gothic nave, was first mentioned in a charter of Henry I. To visit the church and village just follow the lane, then bear left along the High Street to the school

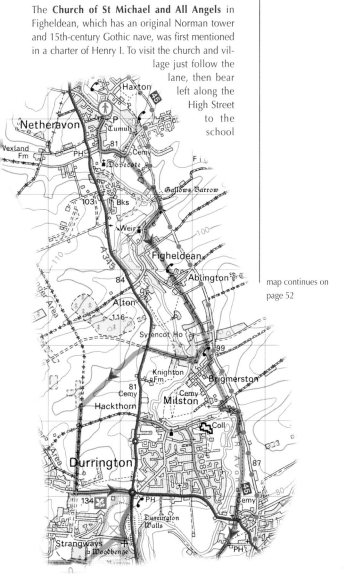

map continues on page 52

49

The Great Stones Way passing through fields at Ablington

and fork left along Avon Banks to rejoin the Great Stones Way at SU 157 468.

Follow the lane for 200m, fork left up through the trees and bear right along the path with the fence on the left, soon passing allotments and houses. Cross the minor road (Pollen Lane) and pass just left of the village hall and recreation area. Continue straight on between fields to a track and houses. Keep ahead down to a lane in **Ablington** opposite the entrance to Ablington Farm.

Turn right and continue for 10m and then go left through a gate. Keep ahead through the field, following the wall on the right at first. Leave via a stile and cross straight over the track (alternative permissive route: continue along the lane, then left following the track past farm buildings, curving left to the stile on the left and turn right). Continue south-south-east along the tree-shaded muddy track. Later cross a driveway and continue through trees to a grassy track. Cross slightly to the right, and continue past the marker post and across the grass to a crossing tank track (SU 162 460). ◄

Here the Great Stones Way and the optional Stonehenge loop go separate ways.

To stay with the Great Stones Way, cross over the track and continue through the field and then between houses to a road at **Brigmerston**. Turn right and continue for 25m, and then go left on a path with woods on the right. Later keep straight on across two fields separated by a stile and leave over another stile. Turn right down the lane and then left just before the corner, cross the **River Avon** and turn left. Cross the river again and follow the lane up past two thatched cottages. As the lane curves left, fork right on a path through the trees.

Cross a stile and take the right-hand fork straight on through the field, cross a stile and continue to cross another stile. Bear right along the field edge and then along the track – later Church Lane – to a main road (A3028) in **Bulford** beside the picturesque 12th-century St Leonard's Church with its squat tower. Across the road and right is the 17th-century Bulford Manor, and 200m to the left is the Rose and Crown pub (01980 638633).

Cross over, go through a gate and past trees, then over a footbridge and bear right through trees. Cross

St Leonard's Church, Bulford

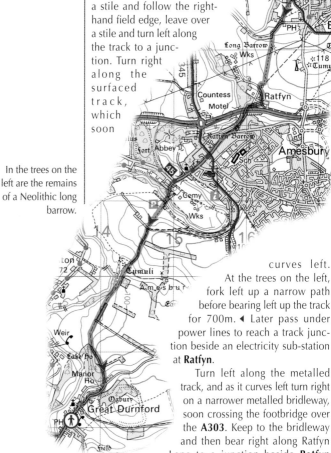

a stile and follow the right-hand field edge, leave over a stile and turn left along the track to a junction. Turn right along the surfaced track, which soon

In the trees on the left are the remains of a Neolithic long barrow.

curves left. At the trees on the left, fork left up a narrow path before bearing left up the track for 700m. ◀ Later pass under power lines to reach a track junction beside an electricity sub-station at **Ratfyn**.

Turn left along the metalled track, and as it curves left turn right on a narrower metalled bridleway, soon crossing the footbridge over the **A303**. Keep to the bridleway and then bear right along Ratfyn Lane to a junction beside **Ratfyn Barrow** (this Bronze Age round barrow is hidden behind the fence – private). Turn right down London Road to the crossroads in **Amesbury**. ◀ Keep ahead (south-west) along the High Street, passing several pubs, the museum and the church.

Anyone returning from Stonehenge to avoid crossing the A303 rejoins the main route here.

52

*Queensberry Bridge
at Amesbury*

The small town of **Amesbury**, tucked in a bend of the River Avon to the east of Stonehenge, has a history stretching back 9000 years to the Mesolithic period. More recently Queen Elfreda founded an abbey here in AD979, and the present Norman Church of St Mary and St Melor originally formed the abbey church. To learn more about the town's history call in at the Amesbury Museum and Heritage Centre. The 'Amesbury Archer' was an early Bronze Age man from 2300BC, whose grave was discovered in Amesbury in 2002. The name 'archer' was coined due to the large number of arrowheads that were buried with him.

Overlooking the town, from a defensive position to the north-west, are the tree-shrouded earthworks of Vespian's Camp, a former Iron Age hill fort (although the area was used during the Neolithic and Mesolithic periods). Below the hill fort, The Avenue – an ancient processional route to Stonehenge – sets out from beside the River

Avon; recent excavations led to the discovery of the remains of a Neolithic henge and stone circle here. Just to the south-east is Boscombe Down Airfield, used for military aircraft research since 1939. And for all Beatles fans, the 'Fab Four' stayed at the Antrobus Arms Hotel in Amesbury in 1965 while filming scenes from their film *Help!*.

Cross the **River Avon** on the footbridge beside the 18th-century Queensberry Bridge and continue to the corner. Bear left up Recreation Road, and just before the car park (SU 149 411) turn right down the enclosed path. Cross three footbridges and bear left along right-hand riverbank for 30m before turning right past a house. Continue up between fences to a four-way track junction.

Go straight on downhill, pass through a gate and follow the left-hand hedge uphill. Keep ahead at the junction, continue across the field and then go alongside the right-hand hedge to a gate in the corner, with the River Avon valley on the right. Continue along the enclosed track and ignore the crossing track. At the next track junction bear left, keeping Ham Wood on the right, and drop

St Andrew's Church Great Durnford

down to a lane beside a house. ▶ Bear right along the lane through **Great Durnford**, keeping left at the bottom of the hill to reach The Black Horse (01722 782270). Along the way a lane on the right leads to the 11th-century Church of St Andrew.

On the hill opposite is Ogbury Camp, a former Iron Age hill fort.

map continues on page 59

Stonehenge loop

At the crossing tank track (SU 162 460) turn right downhill, cross the **River Avon** and keep ahead. Cross the **A345**, continue for 50m and fork half-left (south-west) following a path across the open grass field to a track (byway) at the corner of Stonehenge Firs. Turn left, following the track south for 1.1km to a road junction (parking – SU 144 441); to the right is Larkhill and left is Durrington. Turn left (pavement) to a **roundabout**, circle clockwise across two roads and follow the third (**A345**) south for 250m. Turn right, crossing the road with care, and take the path opposite heading south-west, veering away from the road and soon following the old road, with

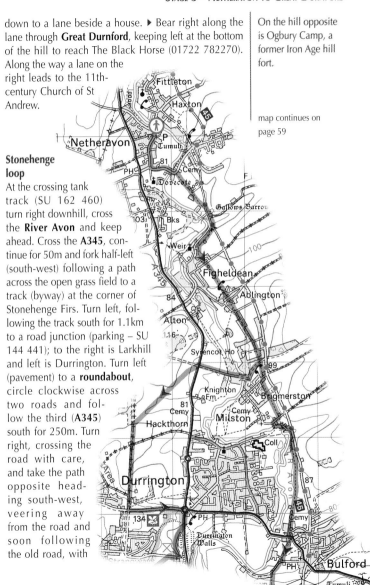

Concrete blocks mark the position of timber posts that once formed Woodhenge

Later a gate on the right allows entry to the open-access site.

Durrington Walls on the right. ◄ At the road (parking SU 151 434) turn right, and just after **Woodhenge** (left) turn half-left through a gate (the gate on the right gives access to Durrington Walls).

> **Durrington Walls** is the site of a large Neolithic henge, around 500m in diameter. Recent excavations found evidence for hundreds of houses dating from 2600BC, making it possibly the largest Neolithic settlement in the whole of northern Europe. Just to the south is **Woodhenge**, which dates from 2300BC. This originally consisted of six concentric upright timber circles that are now marked with concrete markers.

Part-way across and 200m west is the Cuckoo Stone, once a sarsen standing stone, but now fallen over (SU 146 433).

Continue diagonally south-west across the field and leave through a gate in corner. ◄ Turn right along the track-bed of the former Amesbury to Larkhill military railway. After 150m fork slightly left to follow an enclosed path in the same direction, soon with houses on the right, to a cross-track junction at King Barrow Ridge. Straight on is a view of The Cursus.

> Built between 3600 and 3400BC (early Neolithic), **The Cursus** consists of a long rectangular earthwork (bank with external ditch) about 100m wide that runs for 2.8km, roughly on an east–west alignment.

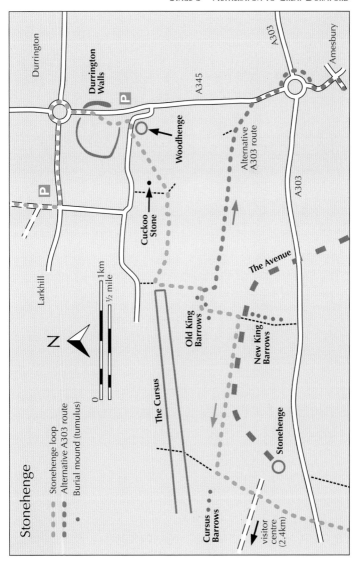

Stonehenge

- ○○○○○ Stonehenge loop
- ●●●●● Alternative A303 route
- ▬ ▬ ▬ Burial mound (tumulus)

The iconic outline of Stonehenge

Take a short detour straight on to view the New King Barrows, a well-preserved collection of early Bronze Age burial mounds.

Turn left along the track (bridleway) to a junction (SU 137 428) and go right through a gate. Follow the track as it goes left at Old King Barrows, passing a copse to reach a gate on the right (SU 134 424). ◀

Turn right through the gate and head generally westwards through two fields separated by a gate. To the south-west is the magical outline of Stonehenge. At the end of the second field go through a gate (SU 121 426) and turn left along the track (byway) for 900m, passing to the right of **Stonehenge**, to reach the **A303**.

The area surrounding **Stonehenge** (designated a World Heritage Site along with Avebury) is littered with prehistoric remains, including several Neolithic long barrows and over 300 early Bronze Age round barrows. The Avenue (an ancient processional route), which dates from between 2600 and 2200BC, runs between Stonehenge and the River Avon at West Amesbury, where a small henge was discovered in 2008. The Avenue's final approach to Stonehenge is aligned with the midsummer sunrise.

Stonehenge itself, which started out as a henge monument some 5000 years ago, was developed in several phases spanning hundreds of years. The large sarsen stones probably came from the Marlborough Downs (passed in Stage 2), whereas the smaller 'bluestones' mostly came from the Preseli Hills in south-west Wales, some 250km away. As for its purpose, there are plenty of theories but no-one really knows. To learn more, call in at the visitor centre (0870 333 1181) located at Airman's Corner, 2.4km west-north-west from the stone circle.

Alternative route to avoid crossing the A303

From **Stonehenge** retrace your steps to the junction at SU 137 428 and turn right. Follow the track as it curves left to reach the A345. Cross over and turn right following the pavement, go through the pedestrian underpass at the A303 roundabout and continue alongside the A345 (pavement) to the crossroads in **Amesbury** (SU 154 416). Turn right along the High Street and follow the main Great Stones Way to Great Durnford (this adds 4km, 70m ascent and 1hr to the Stonehenge loop values).

With great care cross the **A303** and follow the track

After crossing the
A303 the Stonehenge
Loop heads across
Normanton Down

opposite for 400m to a fingerpost. Turn left through a gate
following a permissive path alongside the fence to a track
and turn right over **Normanton Down**; on the right is an
RSPB nature reserve (no access).

Continue down the wide grassy strip and later bear
left along the track towards **Springbottom Farm**. Just after
the barn, fork right on a track (byway) for 1.6km, with
trees on the right at first, and then continue between
fields before later curving left towards **Lake**. At the fingerpost (SU 129 388) signposted 'Great Durnford ¾', turn
right between fences up to the trees and bear left uphill.
Cross a stile and keep ahead beside the boundary. To the
left is a view of the 16th-century Lake House (country
retreat of musician Sting and his wife).

Go over the stile at the corner, cross the minor road
and take the bridleway opposite heading south (thatched
cottage on left). Continue downhill, ignoring a cross-
track, to a path junction beside the **River Avon** (SU 132
379). The Great Stones Way joins from the left, having
just passed through Great Durnford, and heads up the
slight slope into a field. To end in **Great Durnford**, turn
left across the river, follow the path past Durnford Mill
then along the drive to a road, and turn left for 50m to
The Black Horse.

STAGE 6

Great Durnford to Old Sarum (or Salisbury)

Start	Great Durnford – The Black Horse pub (SU 134 379)
Finish	Old Sarum (SU 140 326)
Alternative finish	Salisbury Cathedral (SU 142 296)
Distance	6.8km (4¼ miles) or (Salisbury Cathedral) 10.4km (6½ miles)
Ascent	145m or (Salisbury Cathedral) 155m
Time	2hrs or (Salisbury Cathedral) 3hrs
Maps	OS Explorer 130
Refreshments	Pubs at Great Durnford, Upper Woodford and Old Sarum; lots of choices in Salisbury
Public transport	Old Sarum (SU 141 324) has bus links to Salisbury and Swindon (X5); Salisbury has rail and bus connections
Accommodation	Great Durnford and Salisbury

The final section continues south from Great Durnford to the impressive earthworks of Old Sarum, marking the end of the Great Stones Way. From here you can make your way home or extend the walk to finish at Salisbury Cathedral, one of Britain's finest medieval cathedrals that has stood for over 750 years. For those with time, it would be quite easy to spend a day in Salisbury exploring this historic city.

From The Black Horse (01722 782270) in **Great Durnford** follow the road south-westwards for 50m and turn right

The peaceful River Avon at Upper Woodford

The Stonehenge loop joins from the right here.

along the gravel drive to Durnford Mill. Follow the path across footbridges to a junction on the west side of the **River Avon** (SU 132 379). ◄

Go half-left up the slope to enter a field and follow the left-hand boundary, later continuing between hedges to a track. Bear left (straight on) along the track, which later curves right to the main street in **Upper Woodford**. Turn left, and after passing The Bridge at Woodford pub (01722 782323) turn left across the **River Avon**.

Follow the road through **Netton** for 1.1km, keeping right at three junctions, and just after the right-hand bend and last house on the left, drop down slightly and turn left into the trees. Continue southwards up through the wood, passing under the power lines. Leave through a gate and follow the right-hand

map continues on page 64

field margin to a track beside a seat with a view across the valley.

Turn left uphill for 150m and then right through a gate, following the right-hand field margin. Go through a gate and continue through the small copse, ignoring the crossing **Monarch's Way**, before heading across the field and then descending a track to a junction beside a thatched cottage (Keeper's Cottage; SU 131 345). Keep ahead uphill with trees on the right, then go past a wood (left) to reach an open field. ▸

Ahead the massive earth ramparts of Old Sarum can be seen.

Follow the track, later with trees on the right, and drop down to buildings at Shepherds Corner; continue straight on to a minor road. Cross over and take the fenced bridleway opposite for 400m, with the earthworks up to the right, and go through two gates to join the Old Sarum access road. ▸ Turn right up the access road to visit **Old Sarum** (car park SU 140 326) – the official end of the Great Stones Way. On the way pass a gate on the left beside the outer ramparts; for walkers continuing to Salisbury, this is where the route starts from.

For bus connections head left down to the A345, cross over and turn right for 300m (passing The Old Castle pub, 01722 328703) to the bus stop, or turn left for the Beehive Park and Ride site (700m).

The ruins of the former castle at Old Sarum have a commanding view

Old Sarum, originally established as an Iron Age hill fort around 400BC, became the Roman town of Sorviodunum following the Roman invasion of AD43. Little is known about the site during the Saxon period. However, following the Norman Conquest of 1066, William the Conqueror quickly realised its potential and built the large motte within the earthworks, onto which was built a castle, the remains of which are open to the public (01722 335398). In the late 11th century a cathedral was built within the earthworks. However, its life was short as a new cathedral (the present one) was built in Salisbury, and the one at Old Sarum was later demolished. The castle and associated buildings were finally abandoned during the reign of Henry VIII, although Old Sarum lived on as one of the 'rotten boroughs' and continued to elect members of Parliament until 1832.

Extension to Salisbury

After admiring the remains at **Old Sarum** head back down the access road, passing through the outer rampart, and turn right through a gate. Follow the path, which soon curves left between hedges, and shortly before the **A345** turn right on a path following the right-hand field edge for 150m. Shortly before the corner bear left across the field, go down some steps and turn right (south-west) down the shaded bridleway to a road in **Stratford sub Castle**.

Bear right (straight on) along the road, and at the right-hand bend turn left across the road and follow the metalled foot and cycle path (route 45 – 'City Centre 1') for 900m, soon with the Avon Valley Local Nature Reserve on the right. Just after the leisure centre turn right across the access road (Hulse Road) and continue over a footbridge. Turn left along the metalled cycle

path, cross the road and continue along the riverside route, passing under the **A36** and the **railway**. Turn left across the footbridge and continue along the riverside path. Soon detour round The Boathouse pub before continuing beside the river for 300m. Bear right through an archway and cross a footbridge beside The Mill (pub) to join Bridge Street opposite The King's Head Inn. ▸

The route to Salisbury follows riverside paths

Cross over and continue along the riverside path, with the river on the right, before turning left along Crane Street to a crossroads. Turn right along the High Street, pass through the ancient gateway and keep ahead to the **cathedral** in the centre of The Close and the end of the walk.

The rail station is signposted to the right (700m). For the bus station go left, bear left along Minster Street, then right on Blue Boar Row and left along Queens Street (450m).

> The early 13th-century **Salisbury Cathedral** was built over a short period of time using a single architectural style known as Early English Gothic. This makes it unique among medieval English cathedrals, which typically display several architectural styles. The cathedral, which houses many treasures, also has Britain's tallest spire (123m). Climb the 332 steps for a panoramic view (01722 555120).

The magnificent medieval cathedral at the heart of Salisbury marks the end of the walk

The city of **Salisbury** offers a full range of facilities and numerous interesting sites. Within The Close, in addition to the impressive cathedral, there are the 18th-century Mompesson House, a perfect example of Queen Anne architecture (01722 335659); Arundells, once the home of former Prime Minister Sir Edward Heath (01722 326546); the Salisbury and South Wiltshire Museum, which gives fascinating insights through several thousand years of history (01722 332151); and The Rifles (Berkshire and Wiltshire) Museum (01722 419419).

APPENDIX A

Route summary table

Main stages

Stage	Start	Finish	Distance	Ascent	Time	Page
1	Coate Water (SU 177 827)	Barbury Castle (SU 157 760)	11.3km (7 miles)	245m	3¼hrs	19
2	Barbury Castle (SU 157 760)	Overton Hill (SU 118 680)	10.5km (6½ miles)	80m	2¾hrs	25
3	Overton Hill (SU 118 680)	Casterley Camp (SU 112 536)	18.9km (11¾ miles)	330m	5¼hrs	32
4	Casterley Camp (SU 112 536)	Netheravon (SU 147 490)	8.4km (5¼ miles)	100m	2¼hrs	44
5	Netheravon (SU 147 490)	Great Durnford (SU 134 379)	13.9km (8¾ miles)	220m	4hrs	48
6	Great Durnford (SU 134 379)	Old Sarum (SU 140 326)	6.8km (4¼ miles)	145m	2hrs	61
Total			69.8km (43½ miles)	1120m	19½hrs	

Variant sections

Stage	Variant	Distance	Ascent	Time	Page
2	Avebury loop	3.6km (2¼ miles)	35m	1hr	27
3	Wansdyke and Alton Barnes White Horse route	2.4km (1½ miles)	50m	½hr	33
3	Marden Henge route	1.2km (¾ mile)	-15m	¼hr	39
3	White Horse Trail route	2.1km (1¼ miles)	5m	½hr	41
5	Stonehenge loop	4.2km (2½ miles)	25m	1hr	54
6	Extension to Salisbury	3.6km (2¼ miles)	10m	1hr	64

Notes

Marden Henge route (ascent): **minus** 15m from the ascent figure for Stage 3.

If not following the standard route on Stage 3, walkers will take **either** the Marden Henge route **or** the White Horse Trail route.

APPENDIX B
Useful contact information

The Great Stones Way
www.greatstonesway.org.uk

The Friends of the Ridgeway
www.ridgewayfriends.org.uk

Tourist information
Visit Wiltshire
www.visitwiltshire.co.uk

Salisbury
Fish Row
Salisbury
SP1 1EJ
01722 342860

Swindon
Central Library
Regent Circus
Swindon
SN1 1QG
01793 466454

Public transport information
For train enquiries contact:
National Rail
08457 484950
www.nationalrail.co.uk

Traveline is the best resource for
checking bus timetables:
Traveline
0871 2002233
www.traveline.info

Other contacts
English Heritage
0870 333 1181
www.english-heritage.org.uk

National Trust
0844 800 1895
www.nationaltrust.org.uk

North Wessex Downs AONB
01488 685440
www.northwessexdowns.org.uk

Ramblers Association
020 7339 8500
www.ramblers.org.uk

Wiltshire Wildlife Trust
01380 725670
www.wiltshirewildlife.org

**For sick, injured or distressed animals
and birds**
RSPCA
0300 1234 999

APPENDIX C
Facilities near the route

Stage	Place	Shop	Pub/café	Accommodation	PO	Bus	Train	Toilet
1	Swindon	Y	Y	2, 3	Y	Y	Y	Y
1	Coate Water		Y			Y		Y
1	Chiseldon	Y	Y	2, 3		Y		
1/2	Barbury Castle							Y
2	Avebury	Y	Y	2		Y		Y
2	Avebury Trusloe			2		Y		
2	Beckhampton		Y	2		Y		
2	West Overton		Y			Y		
2/3	East Kennett			2		Y		
3	Honeystreet		Y	1				
3	Bottlesford		Y	3				
3	Wilcot		Y	1, 2				
3	North Newnton		Y	1		Y		
3	Rushall			2		Y		
3/4	Upavon	Y	Y	3	Y	Y		
4	East Chisenbury		Y	3				

Stage	Place	Shop	Pub/café	Accommodation	PO	Bus	Train	Toilet
4	Enford					Y		
4	Longstreet		Y					
4/5	Netheravon	Y	Y		Y	Y		
4/5	Haxton			2				
5	Durrington	Y	Y	2		Y		
5	Larkhill	Y	Y		Y	Y		
5	Bulford	Y	Y	3		Y		
5	Amesbury	Y	Y	2, 3	Y	Y		Y
5/6	Great Durnford		Y	3				
6	Upper Woodford		Y					
6	Old Sarum		Y			Y		Y
6	Salisbury	Y	Y	1, 2, 3	Y	Y	Y	Y

Notes

Accommodation: 1 = campsite or hostel; 2 = B&B; 3 = pub with rooms (including hotel)

Bus services may be limited and/or irregular, and may not operate on Sundays.

No water taps along the route

APPENDIX D
Accommodation near the route

Swindon (near Coate Water)
Holiday Inn
0871 942 9079
www.ihg.com

Goddard Arms
01793 619090

Chiseldon
Rosendale B&B
01793 740726
www.rosendale.biz

The Patriot Arms
01793 740331

Chiseldon House Hotel
01793 741010
www.chiseldonhouse.com

Avebury
Avebury Lodge B&B
01672 539023
www.aveburylodge.co.uk

Manor Farm B&B
01672 539294
www.manorfarmavebury.com

Avebury Trusloe
Aveburylife B&B
01672 539644
www.aveburylife.com

Beckhampton
Beckhampton B&B
01672 539534
www.aveburyworld.co.uk

East Kennett
Old Forge B&B
01672 861686
www.theoldforge-avebury.co.uk

Honeystreet
Campsite at The Barge Inn
01672 851705
www.the-barge-inn.com

Well Cottage B&B
01672 851577
www.well-cottage.org.uk

Bottlesford
The Seven Stars
01672 851325
www.thesevenstars.co.uk

Wilcot (1.6km off White Horse Trail route)
The Golden Swan (campsite and B&B)
01672 562289
www.thegoldenswan.co.uk

North Newnton (600m off White Horse Trail route)
The Woodbridge Inn (campsite)
01980 630266
www.woodbridgeinnpewsey.co.uk

Rushall (2.3km off route)
Rushall Manor B&B
01980 630301
www.rushallmanor.com

Upavon (2.6km off route)
The Antelope
01980 630025
www.antelopeupavon.co.uk

East Chisenbury (1.5km off route)
Red Lion and Troutbeck Guest House
01980 671124
www.redlionfreehouse.com

Haxton (300m off route)
The Old Post Office B&B
01980 671640
www.theoldpostoffice-wiltshire.co.uk

Durrington
Willow Springs B&B
01980 555151
www.willowsprings.co.uk

Melbury House B&B
01980 653151
www.melburyhouse.net

Bulford
Rose and Crown
01980 638633
www.roseandcrown-bulford.co.uk

Amesbury
Antrobus Arms Hotel
01980 623163
www.antrobusarmshotel.co.uk

Fairlawn House B&B
01980 622103
www.fairlawnhotel.co.uk

George Hotel
01980 622108
www.georgehotel-amesbury.com

Mandalay Guest House
01980 623733
www.mandalayguesthouse.com

Great Durnford
The Black Horse
01722 782270

Salisbury
Numerous choices including a youth hostel

NOTES

DOWNLOAD THE ROUTE
IN GPX FORMAT

All the stages of the route are available for download from:

www.cicerone.co.uk/member

as GPX files. You should be able to load them into most formats of mobile device, whether GPS or smartphone.

When you go to this link, you will be asked for your email address and where you purchased the guide, and have the option to subscribe to the Cicerone e-newsletter.

The Great Outdoors

DIGITAL EDITIONS
30-DAY
FREE TRIAL

- Substantial savings on the newsstand price and print subscriptions
- Instant access wherever you are, even if you are offline
- Back issues at your fingertips

Downloading **The Great Outdoors** to your digital device is easy, just follow the steps below:

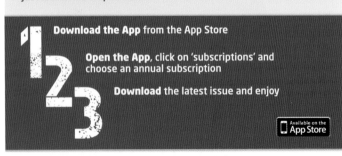

1   **Download the App** from the App Store

2   **Open the App**, click on 'subscriptions' and choose an annual subscription

3   **Download** the latest issue and enjoy

Available on the **App Store**

The digital edition is also available on

The 30-day free trial is not available on Android or Pocketmags and is only available to new subscribers

LISTING OF CICERONE GUIDES

Tour of the Queyras
Tour of the Vanoise
Trekking in the Vosges and Jura
Vanoise Ski Touring
Via Ferratas of the French Alps
Walking in Corsica
Walking in the Auvergne
Walking in the Cathar Region
Walking in the Cevennes
Walking in the Dordogne
Walking in the Haute Savoie – North & South
Walking in the Languedoc
Walking in the Tarentaise and Beaufortain Alps

GERMANY

Germany's Romantic Road
Hiking and Biking in the Black Forest
Walking in the Bavarian Alps
Walking the River Rhine Trail

HIMALAYA

Annapurna
Bhutan
Everest
Garhwal and Kumaon
Langtang with Gosainkund and Helambu
Manaslu
The Mount Kailash Trek
Trekking in Ladakh
Trekking in the Himalaya

ICELAND & GREENLAND

Trekking in Greenland
Walking and Trekking in Iceland

IRELAND

Irish Coastal Walks
The Irish Coast to Coast Walk
The Mountains of Ireland

ITALY

Gran Paradiso
Sibillini National Park
Stelvio National Park
Shorter Walks in the Dolomites
Through the Italian Alps
Trekking in the Apennines
Trekking in the Dolomites
Via Ferratas of the Italian Dolomites: Vols 1 & 2
Walking in Abruzzo
Walking in Sardinia
Walking in Sicily
Walking in the Central Italian Alps
Walking in the Dolomites
Walking in Tuscany
Walking in Umbria
Walking on the Amalfi Coast
Walking the Italian Lakes

MEDITERRANEAN

Jordan – Walks, Treks, Caves, Climbs and Canyons
The Ala Dag
The High Mountains of Crete
The Mountains of Greece
Treks and Climbs in Wadi Rum
Walking in Malta
Western Crete

NORTH AMERICA

British Columbia
The Grand Canyon
The John Muir Trail
The Pacific Crest Trail

SOUTH AMERICA

Aconcagua and the Southern Andes
Hiking and Biking Peru's Inca Trails
Torres del Paine

SCANDINAVIA

Walking in Norway

SLOVENIA, CROATIA AND MONTENEGRO

The Islands of Croatia
The Julian Alps of Slovenia
The Mountains of Montenegro
Trekking in Slovenia
Walking in Slovenia: The Karavanke

SPAIN AND PORTUGAL

Costa Blanca: West
Mountain Walking in Southern Catalunya
The Mountains of Central Spain
The Northern Caminos
Trekking through Mallorca
Walking in Madeira
Walking in Mallorca
Walking in Menorca
Walking in the Algarve
Walking in the Cordillera Cantabrica
Walking in the Sierra Nevada
Walking on Gran Canaria
Walking on La Gomera and El Hierro
Walking on La Palma
Walking on Tenerife
Walking the GR7 in Andalucia
Walks and Climbs in the Picos de Europa

SWITZERLAND

Alpine Pass Route
Central Switzerland
The Bernese Alps
The Swiss Alps
Tour of the Jungfrau Region
Walking in the Valais
Walking in Ticino
Walks in the Engadine

TECHNIQUES

Geocaching in the UK
Indoor Climbing
Lightweight Camping
Map and Compass
Mountain Weather
Moveable Feasts
Outdoor Photography
Polar Exploration
Rock Climbing
Sport Climbing
The Book of the Bivvy
The Hillwalker's Guide to Mountaineering
The Hillwalker's Manual

MINI GUIDES

Alpine Flowers
Avalanche!
Navigating with a GPS
Navigation
Pocket First Aid and Wilderness Medicine
Snow

MOUNTAIN LITERATURE

8000m
A Walk in the Clouds
Unjustifiable Risk?

For full information on all our guides, books and eBooks, visit our website: **www.cicerone.co.uk**.

Walking – Trekking – Mountaineering – Climbing – Cycling

Over 40 years, Cicerone have built up an outstanding collection of 300 guides, inspiring all sorts of amazing adventures.

Every guide comes from extensive exploration and research by our expert authors, all with a passion for their subjects. They are frequently praised, endorsed and used by clubs, instructors and outdoor organisations.

All our titles can now be bought as **e-books** and many as iPad and Kindle files and we will continue to make all our guides available for these and many other devices.

Our website shows any **new information** we've received since a book was published. Please do let us know if you find anything has changed, so that we can pass on the latest details. On our **website** you'll also find some great ideas and lots of information, including sample chapters, contents lists, reviews, articles and a photo gallery.

It's easy to keep in touch with what's going on at Cicerone, by getting our monthly **free e-newsletter**, which is full of offers, competitions, up-to-date information and topical articles. You can subscribe on our home page and also follow us on **Facebook** and **Twitter**, as well as our **blog**.

Cicerone – the very best guides for exploring the world.

CICERONE

2 Police Square Milnthorpe Cumbria LA7 7PY
Tel: 015395 62069 info@cicerone.co.uk
www.cicerone.co.uk